Enacting the Word

Enacting the Word

Using Drama in Preaching

James O. Chatham

Westminster John Knox Press
LOUISVILLE • LONDON

Book design by Teri Vinson
Cover design by Kathy York
Cover art by Laura DeSantis, courtesy of Artville

First edition
Published by Westminster John Knox Press
Louisville, Kentucky

This book is printed on acid-free paper that meets the American National Standards Institute Z39.48 standard. ♾

PRINTED IN THE UNITED STATES OF AMERICA

02 03 04 05 06 07 08 09 10 11 — 10 9 8 7 6 5 4 3 2 1

Library of Congress Cataloging-in-Publication Data is on file at the Library of Congress, Washington, D.C.

ISBN 0-664-22570-5

To the members of

Highland Presbyterian Church,
Louisville, Kentucky,

whose faithful ears and hearts
turned these scripts into a community's worship

Contents

Introduction   1

1 The Word of the Lord Came to Jonah   5

2 God Re-creates   17

3 Rahab   25

4 Persistence in Prayer   31

5 The Call   37

6 Those Who Call Light Darkness and Darkness Light   43

7 He Is Risen!   55

8 Additional Suggestions   65

Introduction

Somewhere in your congregation, there is acting talent. It may not have been used since the high school play, but it is there. Consider inviting that talent to participate in preaching a sermon. Your request will be intimidating at first; the people you ask will not be sure they are adequate for it. But they will also appreciate it. They will like thinking of themselves as having something they can offer in proclaiming God's word. And, down deep, they will be honored.

If they say yes, you will have just given your church a moment it won't soon forget. The sermon, instead of being a monologue from the pulpit, will envelop the congregation, weaving along pew and aisle, setting your people in the middle. They will sense that what is being depicted is *their life*, because it is. And through this depiction you will proclaim the presence of the living God in their midst.

Sermon drama will engage your people in the story and will proclaim the gospel into that story.

The Bible offers primarily three things. First, it offers *anthropology*. It gives an accurate picture of the people we are: the things we do, the impulses that motivate us, the ways we relate to one another, the demons that possess us, the charities that distinguish us, the difficulties we create for ourselves, and the faith we can muster. Moses and David, Mary and Peter are not ideal pictures of the people we *should be*; they are real pictures of the people we *are*! The Bible understands us well! It depicts us accurately. It knows us sometimes even better than we know ourselves. It is on-target anthropology. This is where sermon drama begins: with the telling of *our story*.

Second, the Bible presents *theology*, the best picture we have of the God who occupies this universe with us. God is Mystery, not comprehended by humanity, high and lifted up, always beyond our view, shrouded in

1

smoke, not available to our inspection. But God has granted revelations: through events, through the words of prophets and proclaimers, through storytellers, and most of all through Jesus Christ. From these revelations, the Bible draws a picture of what God does, how God does it, and the purpose God has in mind. Through the Bible, we get our most definitive picture of the ways and means of God.

Sermon drama explores the dynamic relation between anthropology and theology. It depicts typical human sagas and portrays how God is present.

The third thing the Bible offers is *ethic*. How should we act? To what does God call us? Sermon drama can also deliver this message, but it should do so only after anthropology and theology have been thoroughly explored. Ethic with no larger perspective—that is, immediately jumping to the question, "What should we do?"—quickly degenerates into religious moralism, which is a flagrant misuse of the Bible. Sermon drama, as with all preaching, does its best work not when it is used primarily to admonish people on what they ought to do, but when it is used to portray the human story and to reveal the divine presence.

⚛︎⚛︎⚛︎⚛︎⚛︎

Liturgical drama has a long history. There is evidence that religious dramatic rituals reach back as far as ancient Chinese, Indian, Turkish, and Egyptian cultures. The earliest significant example was the "Abydos Passion Play" developed in Egypt around 2500 B.C.E. Modern religious drama originated in the worship of Dionysus in sixth-century Greece. The earliest form was the dithyramb, an improvised story sung by a choral leader, which evolved into Greek tragedy.

During the early centuries of Christianity, drama was seen as degenerate and was shunned. In the tenth century C.E., however, the church began using drama to depict the events of Holy Week. This led to the development of three kinds of drama in the medieval church: mystery plays, the dramatization of Bible stories such as Abraham and Noah; miracle plays, the dramatization of stories of the Christian saints; and morality plays, dramatizations that taught moral lessons. By the thirteenth century, liturgical drama once again came to be viewed as common and degenerate by Pope Innocent III, who banned it in 1250. It remained largely taboo through the Reformation, through the Puritan era, and, indeed, through the nineteenth century. In the twentieth century, however, liturgical drama has been reintroduced into Protestant liturgy and has been used in numerous congregations.

ᘓᕼᘍᕲᘍᕼᘍᕲᘍᕼᘍᕲ

The kind of sermon drama I want to encourage is not the full-scale liturgical play but, rather, fairly simple interaction between the actors/actresses and the preacher—the kind of drama that can be written by a variety of different people and is within reach of production for several Sabbaths in a year. Sometimes it can be "guerrilla theater," short dramatic clips that simply *occur* in the middle of a sermon and are quickly finished. Sometimes it can be dramatic punctuations that flow in and out of the sermon. Sometimes sermon and drama can be wrapped together into a hardly distinguishable whole. The main point is to keep it simple, so that it does not involve enormous preparation and is well within reach.

I cannot testify enough to the exhilaration and the camaraderie produced by the experience. It brings wonderful instincts and talents out of members of a congregation. It puts the preacher in a very different mode with significant new possibilities for communication. It calls on everyone's imagination to devise the best ways to relate a dramatic script to a church sanctuary. And, most of all, it reaches out and pulls a congregation into the sermon's dynamics. If you have never tried sermon drama in your congregation, challenge yourself to do it!

ᘓᕼᘍᕲᘍᕼᘍᕲᘍᕼᘍᕲ

Note: Special effort may be necessary to try to assure that hard-of-hearing members of the congregation will be able to follow what is being spoken.

Chapter One

The Word of the Lord Came to Jonah

Bible Text: Jonah

Introduction

Jonah and the whale is likely the most humorous story in the Bible. Who will not chuckle as a Jerusalem prophet tries to escape the preaching task God sets before him by quietly sailing off in the wrong direction, hoping God will not notice? God then tracks Jonah's every step, ready to use the most persuasive techniques in the divine arsenal to gain Jonah's obedience. In a massive storm that shakes half the Mediterranean, does not God vastly over-make the point?

Who will not laugh as the salty, seasoned sailors—long the symbol of swarthy manhood—reel helplessly across the deck, unable to have any affect on their plight? They pray frantically to their gods (are these really church people?), desperate to quiet the storm. The scene is a living illustration of the slightly altered maxim: "When the going gets tough, the tough get religious."

Who will not laugh at a huge fish that swallows a man whole, provides the man a three-day accommodation in his gargantuan belly, and then, with temporary indigestion, spits out the man alive onto the seashore? Generations of children have delighted in dancing and play-acting this scene.

And, finally, who will not be amused when a stirring statement by God on the wonders of Nineveh's repentance ends with the strange phrase, "and also much cattle," implying that the repentance has taken hold even in the bovine population?

But, for all its humor, Jonah is also thoroughly serious. Its plot belongs to every age. Here is a man of strong religious faith, a prophet of God. He has preached many times about God's amazing grace and steadfast love, about God's unbounded forgiveness.

But does this mean that a loathsome foreign tyrant who has waged major atrocity against Jonah's nation is to be forgiven? Will not God's retribution fall on those we hate so much? Does God pardon our bitterest adversaries? That is a *very* hard question.

Jonah portrays the struggle we religious people go through with the breadth of God's forgiveness. Our torment can go on for years; we want God to *smash* our enemies, but God accepts their repentance. It is a forgiveness we self-righteous faithful cannot tolerate. What are we to do with it?

Location
Church sanctuary

Participants
Jonah—A rather normal, inconspicuous-looking person, male or female
God—Looking the way God should look, male or female
Preacher—In normal attire at the pulpit
Reader—A lay Bible reader
Harpist—If available; can do without
Organist—Prepared for some unorthodox movements
Pianist/Vocalist (optional)*

Props
A four-foot by four-foot (more or less) raised platform in the front of the sanctuary
Coke crate or kitchen stool
A tree or bush, fashioned from wood or cardboard and placed in a conspicuous but not-in-the-way location in the front of the sanctuary (Jonah will have to be able to sit under the bush)

Enactment

Five minutes or so before the worship begins, Jonah enters and seats him/herself in the midst of the congregation. Jonah takes part fully in the worship, which proceeds in its normal way.

---

*Taped copy of music available by writing to Highland Presbyterian Church, 2108 Highland Ave., Louisville, KY 40204 or by e-mailing them at hpresby@bellsouth.net.

Reader: *(Jonah 2)*

Harpist: *(one quiet verse of "There's a Wideness in God's Mercy")*

Pianist/
Vocalist: *("Listen")*

Listen

Words & Music by
Thomas Stafford

If you lis-ten to God, you nev-er know___ Just what will hap-pen or how things will go.___ May-be it's some-thing you did-n't plan to do.___ And that's when your faith___ will have to see you through. So just lis-ten,___ Lis-ten,___ Lis-ten,___ And go in God's___ way.___

Preacher: Some time around the seventh century B.C.E., a very unusual thing happened.

God enters through a sanctuary door, not flippantly, but also without excessive gravity. Moving along an aisle, God looks over the congregation and begins to call out rather forcefully.

God: Jonah! Jonah! I'm looking for you, Jonah! Where are you? Jonah? I'm looking for you!

God addresses one worshiper seated next to the aisle.

> **God:** Hello! I'm God. And I'm looking for my prophet, Jonah. Have you seen him? Have you seen Jonah?

The worshiper, taken by surprise, stammers briefly and does not know how to reply. Jonah arises slightly and hesitantly from across the sanctuary. God spots Jonah.

> **God:** Ah, there you are, Jonah. I have a job for you.

Jonah stands and looks at God.

> **God:** Put on your best prophetic robe, Jonah, and go at once. The wickedness of the great city of Nineveh has come up before my eyes. They are merciless! They are horrible! They are evil! They spread torture and bloodshed across the earth. They cannot be allowed to go on this way.
>
> You, Jonah, you must go in my name and cry out against them! You must proclaim the word of the Lord in their midst! It doesn't have to be a long sermon. Just walk through the city and stand on several street corners and shout, "Repent! Repent!" That will be quite enough. You don't have to do any more.

Pointing to a particular sanctuary exit, God exhorts.

> **God:** Go, now! Go! It must be done at once. Before they wage further destruction against anyone. My patience with them is consumed. If they will not repent of their violence, I will smite them and erase them from the earth! But they must first be warned! Go, quickly!

Jonah looks at God rather blankly but then begins to climb over congregational knees toward an aisle. God, taking Jonah's movement as an affirmative response, moves toward the door from which she/he entered and exits. Jonah's eyes follow God out the door. When Jonah is certain that God has gone, Jonah heads toward a door in a very different direction from the one God pointed to, looking back to make sure God isn't watching as she/he moves through that door.

**Pianist/
Vocalist:** *("Where Do You Think You're Goin'?")*

Where Do You Think You're Goin'?

Words & Music by
Thomas Stafford

Where do you think you're go - in'? You went the wrong___ way.___

You were gi-ven a di-rec-tion that you did-n't fol-low. Now you're gon - na stray.__

You did-n't do what you were told to do.__ Now it's get-ting the

best of you.__ Where do you think you're go - in'? You went the wrong__ way.___

Preacher: Nineveh, located in the prosperous Tigris river valley, was the scourge of the ancient world. Far more powerful than any other kingdom, it took delight in conquering, pillaging, and torturing its neighbors. City after city had absorbed its devastating blows. Its leaders had no respect whatever for anyone else's culture, for anyone else's religion, for anyone else's life. In one Israelite town, the entire Hebrew population was murdered, buried in a deep pit, and covered with pig bones—a strong statement of Nineveh's contempt for anything sacred.

Israel hated Nineveh! Hated its destructiveness! Hated its enormous wealth! Hated its haughty arrogance! Hated every-thing about the evil giant!

Israel waited for—indeed, longed for—the day of vengeance, the day when God would rip through Nineveh's stone walls, smash its fine buildings, litter its streets with wreckage, cut to pieces its people, dash its infants' heads upon the rocks and bring just revenge for the destruction Nineveh had waged on everyone else.

Jonah, when told by God to preach to Nineveh, went the other way—not toward Nineveh! He took a ship westward from the port city of Jaffa and headed across the Mediterranean.

He did not do this because he was afraid. Fear had nothing to do with it. His reason will emerge.

As the ship proceeded across the Mediterranean, a violent storm blew up and began to toss it back and forth. The ship mounted to the heavens and sank to the depths. It threatened to break into pieces.

The entire ship's crew prayed to their gods to end the storm. They held a prayer meeting right on deck, but the storm only grew worse.

Finally, Jonah, confessing that he was the problem, consented to be thrown overboard. And as soon as he sank under the sea, the storm abated and the sea became calm. We all know where Jonah landed!

Harpist: *(swirling notes, simulating water, up and down, growing and lessening, up and down)*

Jonah emerges from the door he/she left, and swirls and floats toward the raised platform in the front of the sanctuary. Landing on the platform (which represents the belly of the great fish), he/she is stunned for a moment.

Organist: *(begins a succession of low, thumping sounds that simulates the heartbeat of the fish)*

Recovering, Jonah arises and slowly assesses the situation, pantomiming her/his hands around the inner contours of the fish's stomach. Jonah searches for a way out. Realizing that there is none, Jonah sits down to wait.

**Pianist/
Vocalist:**   *("You're Stuck")*

You're Stuck

Words & Music by
Thomas Stafford

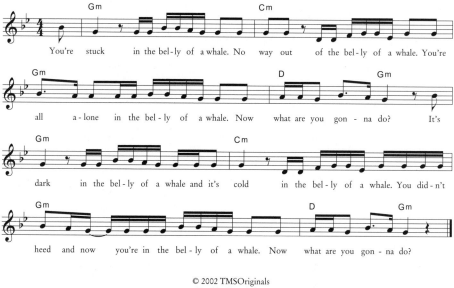

You're stuck in the bel-ly of a whale. No way out of the bel-ly of a whale. You're all a-lone in the bel-ly of a whale. Now what are you gon-na do? It's dark in the bel-ly of a whale and it's cold in the bel-ly of a whale. You did-n't heed and now you're in the bel-ly of a whale. Now what are you gon-na do?

Organist: *(continues whale heartbeat, then backs off the volume)*

Jonah eases over onto his/her knees and prays.

Jonah: The waters have closed over me, O God! The deep is round about me! Sheol has claimed me. Hell itself has closed me in its prison. Rescue my life from the pit, O Lord! Hear my prayer and answer me in my need. I will sing songs of thanksgiving in your holy temple! I will pay all the tithes I have vowed! The right hand of the Lord is strong; deliver me in my need, O God!

Organist: *(The volume of the thumping picks up. Then there is a guttural heaving that builds upward toward a climax [simulating the fish about to vomit]. The climax happens, and the fish's belly heaves.)*

Jonah is spit out onto the seashore. He/she lands on all fours, stunned.

Organist: *(stops)*

Harpist: *(one measure of, "There's a Wideness in God's Mercy")*

Jonah sits up and looks around. God appears.

God: You didn't believe me, did you, Jonah? Well, I'll say it one more time. Get up and go to Nineveh, that city of great wickedness, and proclaim repentance in its streets! You are my prophet, Jonah. How many times do I have to say that to you? Hurry, now, the time is short!

Jonah looks up at God, gets up, straightens him/herself out, looks at God again, and then heads off in the direction God had specified previously—out the door. God exits through God's door.

Preacher: This time, Jonah went to Nineveh. He entered the gates of the city, and he did what God told him to do.

Jonah returns through the same door, carrying an old wooden Coke crate, or some other box of similar size and weight. Jonah moves to one corner of the sanctuary, sets down the crate, stands on it, looks around at the people, and proclaims loudly.

Jonah: Repent!

Jonah picks up the crate, moves to a second corner of the sanctuary, sets it back down and stands on it. He again looks at the people and proclaims loudly.

Jonah: Repent!

Jonah picks up the crate and moves to a third corner of the sanctuary, sets it back down, and stands on it. He again looks out across the people and proclaims loudly.

Jonah: Repent!

Jonah picks up the crate and moves to a fourth corner of the sanctuary, sets it back down, and stands on it. He again surveys the people and proclaims loudly.

Jonah: Repent!

Then Jonah sits down under the bush and gazes at the congregation.

Pianist/
Vocalist: *("Leave This Nightmare Behind")*

Leave This Nightmare Behind

Words & Music by
Thomas Stafford

God enters, looks around at the congregation with great delight, turns toward Jonah, and declares.

God: Wonderful job, Jonah! Wonderful job! They are repenting! Every one of them! Look at them! Can you believe it? The King of Nineveh has taken off his royal robe, and has dressed himself in sack cloth and is sitting in ashes. And the people are following him! Look at them! It's wonderful, Jonah! I will not have to destroy the city after all! I will not have to bring down my hail and lightning and wind and fire against them! I will not have to beat down their buildings and kill their people. They are repenting! A wonderful job you have done here, Jonah!

God looks at Jonah. Jonah scowls, angry! Sullen and hurt, Jonah shouts.

Jonah: I knew you were going to do this, God! That's why I didn't want to come over here in the first place! You're nothing but a soft touch. You forgive everybody! "Slow to anger and abounding in steadfast love"—they sure got you right with that one!

God: That's the trouble with you human beings, Jonah. You want me to be a God of love. But you want to pick the people I'm going to love. And you want to pick others for me to hate!

Jonah: Forgive Nineveh? For god's sake, God, they've never forgiven us! They've tortured us, and burned us, and brutalized us, and murdered us! This, if I may say so, is the most dolt-headed thing you have ever done!

God: You want me to agree with your prejudices! You want me to favor the people you favor and disdain the people you disdain.

Jonah: Don't forgive these nasty people, God! Burn them! They are the curse of the civilized world!

God: And the more religious you are, the more you think you can claim me! All I have to do is put one tiny little touch of faith in your heart and you think you own me!

Jonah: Send the angels of God to slice them in pieces with flaming swords! Throw every lightning bolt you possess at them!

God: "Bless these people over here, God; they are our friends. Curse those over there; they are our enemies."

Jonah: Rain giant hailstones on them! Send ravenous lions to eat them! Let the locusts devour their crops, and the angel of death kill their children!

God: You want to take your seat on my throne and run the whole place! Well, I can't remember that I granted you the prerogative to do that!

Jonah: I'm waiting, God! Bring down justice against this evil city! Give them their full reward for everything they have done!

God: My ways are higher than your ways, Jonah. My thoughts are far above your thoughts. Why should I not show mercy to Nineveh? For I am God, not human, the Holy One in your midst!

God and Jonah look at each other, the conflict not resolved—the conflict is never resolved.

Preacher: "Love your enemies. Pray for those who persecute you," said our Lord. Yes, God's ways *are* higher than our ways, and God's thoughts *are* far above our thoughts—which is the hope of the world. Thanks be to God. Amen.

Jonah sits back in her/his original seat. God leaves through the God door. The preacher sits down.

Harpist: *(a concluding verse of "There's a Wideness in God's Mercy")*

THE END

Chapter Two

God Re-creates

Bible Texts: Psalm 107; 1 Corinthians 15:50–57

Introduction

We Christians have a relatively easy time believing that God is the Creator. The beauty, the complexity, and the intricacy of the universe speak this message richly.

We have a much more difficult time believing that God is the Re-creator. That God can take the seemingly hopeless situations into which we get ourselves and bring from them renewal and vitality. That God can bring life from death.

This is the best news the pulpit has to offer: that God can take the people we have become and re-create new beings. Just as God took a band of Egyptian slaves and made them into a strong nation, just as God collected twelve Galilean peasants and made them a church that would revolutionize history, God can give us new life! We are not consigned to remain always the people we are now. We are not destined simply to continue the present. God hears. God comes. God offers hope, possibility. That is the re-creative power God possesses.

Every week, a couple of hundred alcoholics gather at my church asking the question: "Can I find new life?" Every year, more than 500 refugees flow through our refugee resettlement agency asking the question: "Can I find new life?" With great frequency, I meet with members of my congregation who are struggling with a relationship, a job, or a lifestyle, and who are asking: "Can I live in a new way?" The question is universal. And we come to church hoping that the answer is yes, that this incomprehensible miracle the church preaches is actually true.

What is at stake, of course, is hope. Should we be realistic and give up? Common sense says we should. Or should we, on the other hand, believe that it can actually happen? That the Re-creator can act on us, too?

The drama that follows proclaims the miracle. It shows several very difficult plights we humans get into, and invites us, through the struggle, TO BELIEVE!

⟡⟡⟡⟡⟡⟡

The panels of this drama need not be presented continuously. They can be spaced through a worship service, or interlaced with choral and/or hymn music or with litany that declares the message.

Location
Church sanctuary

Participants
Reader—A lay Bible reader
Preacher—In normal attire at the pulpit
An aging woman
A thoroughly bedraggled alcoholic carrying a bag-with-bottle
Four "voices" spoken from across the congregation
A middle-aged, well-dressed man
An abused spouse
A very young woman carrying a small baby
A vivacious twenty-something

Props
None

Enactment

Reader: *(Psalm 107:1–3)*

Preacher: This morning, there is good news, my friends! The best news in the universe!

God makes all things new! All people new! Who we are is not who we have to be. What is is not what has to come. Sound the trumpet! Issue the proclamation! God's redeeming power reigns in our world! God's creative power re-creates! Christ is risen, and in God's strength, we too are called to rise!

An Aging Woman makes her way onto the stage. She is erect, purposeful, not obviously feeling sorry for herself. But there is also a touch of pathos, a slight hollowness. She addresses the congregation as a close friend, someone she didn't really expect to encounter here today, but as one to whom she relates readily and intimately. She speaks as if she were answering their question, "How are you?" She doesn't intend the whole world to hear, but she feels free to express herself in this relationship.

Aging
woman: *(with a touch of formality)* How am I? Well enough, I guess. Making it. You know: We survive these things. [moving toward intimacy] But let me tell you how it really is. *The day he passed away* [italicized words articulated very clearly, but not over-emphasized], EVERY-THING changed. A HOLE in my life. The house is quiet. The walls don't speak. Everything I do is for me alone. No interaction. No relationship. No laughter. No future to think about together. Fifty-one years is a long time, you know.

And the question I hear myself asking inside is, "Is there anything left? Where do I go now? What's it worth? I don't know what the answer will be. Everybody tries to be nice, but your relationship with people changes drastically. You're one now, not two.

I'm struggling with it. Do you have any advice?

After a moment of pause, the woman leaves the stage.

Preacher: God gives strength to the faint of heart, courage to the weak. "Come unto me, you who labor and are heavy laden! Let your hearts find hope in my power!" The trumpet shall sound, and the dead will be raised! Thanks be to God who gives us this victory through our Lord Jesus Christ.

Music or other parts of the service may occur here.

Reader: *(Psalm 107:4–9)*

Preacher: There is good news, my friends! God makes things new! People new! Who we are is not who we have to be. What is is not what has to come. Sound the trumpet! Issue the proclamation! God's redeeming power reigns in our world! God re-creates! Christ is risen, and we too are called to rise!

A grotesque, disheveled, Alcoholic Man, sunken and bent, enters the sanctuary and makes his way slowly onto the stage. Near the middle, he pauses and peers around. From the congregation, voices shout.

Voice 1: Who is THAT creep?

Voice 2: He looks like some wretched old sot who wandered in here off the street.

Voice 3: He looks terrible! What's he doing up there?

Voice 1: Yeah, get rid of that guy before he desecrates the place.

Voice 4: *(loud, commanding)* What a minute! [brief pause] God sent him here. That guy is who I'll be in five years if I don't stop. I am right on his path. QUITTING—IS—SO—HARD! My mind struggles with it day and night. It seems so harmless just to go have another drink, and it would make me feel SO GOOD! But that man right there is ME if I do.

There has got to be a way out of this! I want to go back to the beginning and start over. Can somebody tell me if that is possible?

The shrunken man peers blankly out at the congregation, and then makes his way to sit beside Voice 4.

Preacher: Struggle hard! Cast off the chains that bind you, the prison that holds you. And know that God walks with you through this valley of the shadow of death. "I have come to preach good news to the poor," Christ says. "Release to the captives, liberty to the oppressed, to proclaim the year of the Lord's favor!" Thanks be to God who gives us this victory through our Lord Jesus Christ.

Music or other parts of the service may occur here.

Reader: *(Psalm 107:10–16)*

Preacher: Good news, my friends! The best news in the universe! God makes all things new! All people new! Who we are is not who we have to be. What is is not what has to come. Sound the trumpet! Issue the proclamation! God's redeeming power reigns in our world! God's creative power re-creates! Christ is risen, and in God's strength, we too are called to rise!

From out of the congregation, a Well-dressed Man rises and comes to the stage. He looks confident, but with a slight tinge of puzzlement.

Well-dressed
man: I was doing really well! Real estate law. I'll tell you, I was good! Lots of work. Lots of money. No end to the opportunities. And a GOOD reward every payday. I was respected. Knew a lot of people. I was SOMEBODY. Made the "Going Up" section of the "Business Weekly."

And then, one day, right in the middle of it all, I stopped and looked around. Seventy hours a week. Never home. Never slow down. Never *ponder*; just *do*.

And no matter how much I work, it's not enough. There's always far more.

And then I asked myself honestly: "Where is this taking me? Is it anywhere I want to go? Is it somewhere I believe in?" And I couldn't find the answer to that question. Came up blank.

And I'm wondering now: Is there something else I want to do with the rest of my life? Can I find what would really make me feel worthwhile?

Well-dressed Man exits the stage and resumes his seat in the congregation.

Preacher: God points direction. God gives strength. Search in the Lord. Thanks be to God who gives us this victory through our Lord Jesus Christ.

Music or other parts of the service may occur here.

Reader: *(Psalm 107:17–22)*

Preacher: Good news, my friends! The best news in the universe! God makes all things new! All people new! Who we are is not who we have to be. What is is not what has to come. Sound the trumpet! Issue the proclamation! God's redeeming power reigns in our world! God's creative power re-creates! Christ is risen, and in God's strength, we too are called to rise!

The Abused Woman moves onto the stage, halting, head bowed, uncertain, genuinely conflicted. More than addressing the congregation, she is addressing herself; the congregation overhears.

Abused
woman: I—HAVE—GOT—TO—LEAVE—HIM! He's violent! He's awful! Bruises all over me! He demands that I hide them, cover them up! That skin powder is the biggest lie I tell! But they still won't hide from me! I know everything!

I live in terror: when will he hit me again? It's awful!

Am I doing something wrong? If I were a better person, would he not be this way?

I'm scared. Really scared! If I leave him, he'll kill me. He'll find me, and that will be the end.

Can I find some better way to live than this? Or am I locked in?

Abused woman leaves the stage.

Preacher: "Come unto me, you who labor and are heavy laden. Let your hearts find strength! Let your lives find healing. I am the Creator, the Re-creator!" Thanks be to God who gives us this victory through our Lord Jesus Christ.

Music or other parts of the service may occur here.

Reader: *(Psalm 107:23–32)*

Preacher: There is good news, my friends! The best news in the universe! God makes all things new! All people new! Who we are is not who we have to be. What is is not what has to come. Sound the trumpet! Issue the proclamation! God's redeeming power reigns in our world! God's creative power re-creates! Christ is risen, and in God's strength, we too are called to rise!

A Young Woman enters the stage carrying a small baby. She looks directly at the congregation.

Young
woman: We were just having fun! It seemed harmless. Nothing was going to happen.

My mother says, "You've got to keep him. You brought him into this world, and he is your responsibility now."

My grandmother says, "We cannot let ANY of our relatives know that this has happened in our family!"

My father says, "It was enough trying to support you; now there's two of you."

My brother says, "Sis, you really want HIM following you around everywhere you go?"

I am confused. Have I ruined my life forever? Is there any hope of getting back to being a teenager?

Girl and baby leave the stage.

Preacher: The people who walked in darkness have seen a great light! Those who dwelt in the land of deep darkness, on them has light shined. God does not leave us desolate. Struggle forward in hope. God can make of us new people! Thanks be to God who gives us this victory through our Lord Jesus Christ.

Music or other parts of the service may occur here.

Reader: *(Psalm 107:33–38)*

Preacher: There is good news, my friends! The best news in the universe! God makes all things new! All people new! Who we are is not who we have to be. What is is not what has to come. Sound the trumpet! Issue the proclamation! God's redeeming power reigns in our world! God's creative power re-creates! Christ is risen, and in God's strength, we too are called to rise!

A Twenty-Something stands on the stage, neat, well dressed, but perplexed. She/he has a problem.

Twenty-something: It happened overnight! Before I knew it! I mean, it was so easy, I hardly even noticed.

Eighteen percent! Have you ever tried to pay off a debt at 18 percent? On MY salary? It's buried in the little print. They don't tell you up front.

"Hello! This is Joe! From the Buy-It-When-You-Want-It Credit Card Company. Great news! You're pre-approved! You can have whatever you want, right now. Why wait? Go ahead! Treat number one. You deserve it!"

Sure! Treat number one now . . . , and then bury yourself in the biggest hole in the universe.

"You MUST return your minimum payment."

"You MUST demonstrate good faith effort to bear your responsibility."

"You MUST pay by April 30."

They didn't haul out any of that MUST language when they were urging me to use the card.

What am I going to do? Is there any hope for getting out of this mess?

Twenty-something exits.

Preacher: Release for the captive. A future for the confused. A way for the lost. Thanks be to God who gives us this victory through our Lord Jesus Christ.

Reader: *(Psalm 107:39–43)*

THE END

Chapter Three

Rahab

Bible Texts: Joshua 2; Matthew 1:1–16

Introduction

Rahab is a prostitute who runs a brothel in Jericho. A hardened creature, she is cynical about her clients, about her city, about herself. She is visited one day by two strangers from the desert, spies from a small, itinerant people called Israel.

Israel has recently escaped slavery in Egypt through the parted waters of the Red Sea. They are encamped during this story in the Sinai Desert at Shittim. They are traveling across Sinai toward the land of Canaan, which, they understand, God has promised to give them. Their plan is to conquer and settle Canaan. In preparation for the conquest, Israel has sent these two spies to search out the land, to assess the challenge it poses. The spies go to Jericho, a town just inside Canaan protected by a massive stone wall. Slipping into the city by day while the gates are open, they do their intelligence work. Then, as evening approaches, they go to the house of Rahab to spend the night. From there, the story develops.

๑ใๅ๑ใๅ๑ใๅ๑

This story participates in two major Biblical themes. The first theme is the faithfulness of God. In the genealogy at the beginning of his Gospel, Matthew (Matt. 1:1–16) charts forty-one generations from Abraham to Jesus. His apparent purpose is to proclaim that the God who promised prolific progeny, a permanent homeland, and continued blessing to Abraham (Gen. 12:1–3) has been faithful over forty-one generations in fulfilling that promise in Jesus the Christ. God is "from everlasting to everlasting" (Ps. 90:2), and God's promises span the same era, never falling void. Matthew includes in the genealogy "Salmon the father of Boaz by Rahab" (Matt. 1:5), an historically impossible construct, but part of Matthew's proclamation of the faithfulness of God. Through Rahab, God worked God's faithfulness.

And that becomes the second theme in the Rahab story: that God can work God's faithfulness through people like her. That God does not always choose those we would choose. That God can select foreigners, sinners, prostitutes, brothel operators. That God's grace is far more gracious than ours, offered to far more people than we would.

Put together, the themes proclaim that God is Wholly Other, very different from us, not to be domesticated into our images, always turning out to be bigger than our theological conclusions.

Location
Church sanctuary

Participants
Preacher—In normal attire at the pulpit

Rahab—A seasoned, surly prostitute, young enough still to be of child-bearing age, but old enough to be hardened and cynical

Spy 1—A worn-looking traveler, just in from the desert

Spy 2—Younger colleague of Spy 1

Jericho Authority 1:—Serious and urgent, justifiably concerned over the current situation that could portend danger

Jericho Authority 2—Under the command of Jericho Authority 1

Props
A small thing amiss inside Rahab's house that she can attend to (such as a towel that needs to be folded)

A rope for descending to the ground from a window

A scarlet cord, thick enough to be visible to the congregation

Enactment

Preacher: Sometime before 1200 B.C.E., something like the following took place.

Rahab ascends center stage. She is inside her house. It is late afternoon, and Jericho is beginning to shut down. She looks this way and that, offhandedly checking to see that her place is in order before evening customers arrive. She sees one small thing that needs correcting and goes over to do it. There are four knocks at the door.

Rahab: Who is it? Come in! It's unlocked!

The door opens. Spy 1 and Spy 2 enter and move, a bit tentatively, toward center stage. They speak politely.

Spy 1: We are travelers seeking lodging, Madame. We have come a long distance, and we are very weary.

Spy 2: May we find lodging in your house?

Rahab: Can it, buster. You know very well what you can find in my house. Why else did you come here? Too long in the desert! That lean and raunchy look! No matter where they come from, once they get in my door, they are all the same. Looking for one thing only! Someone back home would be awfully upset if she knew you were here!

Spy 1: At your pleasure, Madame.

Rahab: It's not my pleasure! It stopped being my pleasure a long time ago. It's your pleasure. To me it's just business, buster. You want to feel good; I want to eat. It's that simple. Did you bring your money?

Spy 2: Well, Madame, you see. . . .

Spy 1: The only thing we bear is the purpose in our hearts. Until now, we have been fed by the ravens and sheltered by the mother eagle.

Rahab: No money! You go tell that mother eagle she better keep working! I don't give free rides. It's beneath my dignity!

There are three sharp knocks at the door.

Rahab: Who is it? Don't tell me you brought the family.

Jericho 1: Jericho Authority. Open up! On the double!

Rahab motions Spy 1 and Spy 2 to hide in a secret place. They hide. Rahab opens the door.

Rahab: Here to close me down again, are you? I'd think you'd be getting tired of this. You fools are bound to have better crooks to chase than me.

Jericho 1: Button it up, Momma. We're not after you. You're small pota-
toes. Two spies are in town. Spotted this afternoon. Looking the
town over. They came here. Checked in at everyone's favorite
motel. Where are they?

Rahab: Spies? Those two? They looked like a couple of hungry bedouin
wolves to me. You sure you're looking for the right people?

Jericho 1: They are not just bedouins. These two had a completely different look. Nothing you'd see around here.

Rahab: Where from, then?

Jericho 2: A tribe down in the Sinai Desert. Israel. They used to be
Pharaoh's slaves in Egypt, but they escaped. Now they're looking
for a place to settle, and we're afraid they're looking here. Where
are they?

Rahab: I let 'em out the same door you just came in. No money, no
accommodation: That's my policy. Last I saw, they headed east
toward the river. If you want 'em, you better hurry. They got
quite a start on you.

Jericho 1: Let's go, Gabe. Nothing here. We better follow the lead. The
chief will be really unhappy if we don't wind this up!

*Jericho 1 and Jericho 2 exit from the same door they entered. Rahab looks behind
them, shuts the door, and then returns to center stage.*

Rahab: Come on out. They're gone.

Spy 1 and Spy 2 emerge.

Rahab: Israel, huh? Serious business. You guys getting ready to take us
over?

Spy 1: Our leaders are asking that question. They think God has
promised us this land.

Rahab: Well, I get a lot of news through here. Is it true what happened
to you people in Egypt? All that Red Sea business, the Egyptians
getting drowned as they chased you?

Spy 2: We wouldn't be here if it weren't true.

Rahab: Awesome! What's going on between God and you people?

Spy 1: We're not sure, but whatever it is is for real.

Rahab: What can I do to help you?

Spy 1: You already have. When the invasion comes, tie this scarlet cord in the window of your house, and we will help you.

Spy 1 and Spy 2 let themselves out the window and down the rope.

Preacher: Rahab, the harlot of Jericho, this surly, cynical woman whose only "dignity" is to get paid for what she does, plays an amazing part in the Biblical story. Not only does God call on her to live a key role in enabling Israel to settle the Promised Land. But she is also listed by Matthew as a grandmother of Jesus, one of the women in Jesus' lineage.

This is astounding! Astounding that Rahab is a central figure in the story of your salvation and mine. Astounding that through this woman of ill repute, blessing flows from heaven to earth.

The world shunned her; God claimed her. The world looked at her and saw evil; God looked at her and saw a servant. Astounding!

Time and again, the Bible wants us to see that God works not only through those we approve of, but also through those we disdain. That God can bless us through Canaanites, through Moabites, through Samaritans, through Jews, through Muslims, through Chinese, through Iranians. "Nothing is impossible with God!" an angel would later speak to Rahab's granddaughter. Rahab herself was a living illustration.

As we move into a new millennium in which we will be called upon to associate with far greater human diversity than ever before, we, Christians, need to listen carefully to what our Bible has been saying for the past two thousand years: that God does not remain confined to the limits we draw. That God created an entire world full of people, and that God works with a great variety of those people in fulfilling the divine promises. That God can choose the likes of Rahab to bless us. We need a theology that allows that.

THE END

Chapter Four

Persistence in Prayer

Bible Text: Luke 18:1–7

Introduction

Here is a poignant story that can be conveyed powerfully in worship by the preacher and two actors. One actor has not-complicated lines to speak, and the other does only movement and facial/body expressions.

Jesus was talking about prayer with his disciples. Luke says that he "told them a parable about their need to pray always and not to lose heart." Losing heart is something we human beings seem especially quick to do. If we don't get results from our endeavor within hours or days, we are strongly tempted to give up. The world counsels us: "Don't keep beating a dead horse." The need for quick-fix solutions seems especially characteristic of our time. God, of course, is "from everlasting to everlasting," and is often not in as big a hurry as we are.

In the story, there is a judge who "neither feared God nor had respect for people." There is also a widow, a symbol of the most powerless person in first-century society. The widow is being harrassed, challenged, by some opponent—we are not told the situation. She comes to the judge asking for justice. The judge refuses to pay her any attention. She returns repeatedly, until the judge finally declares, "Though I have no fear of God and no respect for anyone, yet because this widow keeps bothering me, I will grant her justice, so that she may not wear me out by continually coming." Jesus then asks, If an unrighteous judge finally grants this woman's petition, will not the righteous God all the more give justice to those who ask?

This account reflects a technique often used by first-century Jewish rabbis in making a theological point: If human beings act *this good way*, will not God act the same way but far more so? The parables of reclamation and forgiveness in Luke 15 (lost sheep, lost coin, lost son) are set up according to this model.

I used this drama as the final sermon in a five-part series on prayer. In the first sermon, my associate preached on "the power of prayer," prayer as relationship with God rather than prayer that demands results. In the second, I preached on the Lord's prayer, an illustration presented by Jesus of his exhortation for us to *be private* and to *be brief* when we pray. In the third, I dealt with, "When Prayer Finds No Answer," contending, from the psalms and the passion narrative, that unanswered prayer stands at the center of our faith, not on the periphery. In the fourth, our seminary intern presented a pattern for prayer that has been very helpful and meaningful for him, taken from an analysis of Isaiah 6 by George Buttrick. The following drama closed the series.

Location
Church sanctuary

Participants
Reader—A lay Bible reader
Preacher—In normal attire at the pulpit
The Judge—A rather stern looking older person dressed for business
The Widow—A cleanly dressed, humble middle-age woman

Props
A simple desk, placed at the front of the sanctuary so that the congregation can see mostly its side and loaded with papers and a big thick book or two.
A chair, placed behind the desk and turned slightly to face toward the congregation.
An imaginary door, placed across from the desk and several feet away and demarcated by masking tape on the floor. The face of the door is toward the desk, the edge toward the congregation.

Enactment

Reader: *(Luke 18:1–7)*

Preacher: Jesus told this story. Once there was a judge.

Judge enters, dressed in a business suit, a stern, intent look on his face—not angry but serious. He pauses center stage, surveys the congregation briefly, his face not changing, never showing any trace of warmth. He turns, takes keys from his pocket, and opens

the invisible door. Proceeding through it, he moves to the chair behind a business desk.
He sits down and begins working among the papers on the desk.

Preacher: The judge neither feared God nor had any respect for people. He simply didn't care about either of them. He didn't care about oppression; he didn't care about mercy. He didn't care about justice; he didn't care about injustice. He didn't care about cheating, lying, or stealing. He didn't care about whether God was happy or unhappy. He didn't care about exploitation or manipulation or fraud. He didn't care about what any preacher said during synagogue worship, or what any prophet prophesied from the Temple steps. He didn't care.

There was only one thing this judge cared about: *He wanted to be left alone!* The final word, the definitive wisdom: LEAVE THE JUDGE ALONE! That's all that mattered.

Judge looks up, same facial attitude. He looks around briefly, returns to work.

Widow enters on the opposite side of the stage from the desk. Slowly, cautiously, a bit haltingly. She has a pleasant enough but also determined look on her face that matches the tone of her body. She knows that she is an essentially powerless person, and she knows that she is treading on unfamiliar territory. But she also has a mission. She advances toward the invisible door the judge entered moments before. She stops, surveying it.

Preacher: There was also a widow in that judge's town. The widow had a tormentor, someone who was treating her unjustly. Widows in that ancient time were essentially defenseless. No father to look after them. No husband to protect them. An open target. Anything a widow owned, you could probably get if you were callous enough. Someone was being miserably callous to this widow. She wanted a court judgment to stop it!

Widow taps at the imaginary door.

Judge: *(firmly, in a voice of authority)* Go away!

Judge continues his work. Widow pauses, not determining for the moment what to do next. Then, Widow taps again.

Judge: *(louder, with no exasperation, just authority)* Go away! Don't bother me!

Widow bursts in through the door, lays a paper on the judge's desk, retreats backward through the door, and moves a distance away. Judge glances briefly at the paper, sets it down.

Preacher: This judge really did not want to be bothered! He had no concern for justice, no instinct for mercy, no interest in walking humbly with his God. The only thing he wanted was to be left alone.

Judge works on. Widow moves forward to the door again. She knocks, this time more resolutely.

Judge: (*growing angry, more authoritative*) Woman, I have no interest in you! I don't care about your grievance! I don't care about your stupid rights! I don't care about the court judgment you want! All I care about is that you leave me alone!

Judge continues working. Widow does what she is told. She withdraws from the door and seats herself tentatively at the top of the chancel steps, still looking at the door.

Preacher: You see, this judge was totally serious! He was wound up in his own world! He did not regard either the difficulties of humanity or the wishes of God. He wanted to be left alone! Nothing else. Moses himself, the founder of his profession, could have knocked at that door, and this judge would not have cared. He was not going to answer anybody!

Widow rises, moves to the door, pauses, knocks more loudly. This time, there is a burst of response!

Judge: Wretched woman! Depart out of my sight! Stop that incessant knocking at my door! Leave me alone! Go away! Cease tormenting me! Take your blessed grievance somewhere else! Turn yourself toward the town and disappear in it! Vanish!

Judge returns to work. Widow looks defeated. She withdraws and seats herself on a chair, struggling with her own thoughts.

Preacher: (*walking over and gesturing at the judge—the preacher is an invisible presence whom the judge and the widow are not aware of*) This was the most obstinate judge you have ever seen. He wasn't going to give in to anybody! That widow could have been his mother, and he wouldn't have cared. A stone wall.

(gesturing at door): There was no way anybody was going to get through that door to him.

(walking over and addressing widow): Forget it, lady, your cause is lost! The end! You will have to solve your grievance some other way. There is no mercy behind that door. *(preacher returns to pulpit)*

Widow rises and moves toward the door again. This time, she pounds with her fists, both arms flailing. Judge rises. He stalks toward the door. Grabbing it open, he looks at her and shouts.

Judge: Woman, you are the most impertinent, stubborn, annoying person I have ever met! You will not stop! You pester me without mercy! Okay! Not because I care about you, or God, or justice, or mercy, or anything else. Not because of any compassion in my heart. ONLY TO GET RID OF YOU, to keep you from pounding endlessly on my door—for that and no other reason. . . .

Judge walks to his desk, grabs the piece of paper that the widow left there, scribbles something on it, signs it, returns to the door, and thrusts it at the widow.

Judge: Here! Your vindication! Take it! Be gone! Never pass beneath my sight again!

Widow takes the paper, looks at it, smiles broadly, does a polite bow to speak her thanks, turns, and is gone. Judge, unmoved, turns, walks to his desk, sits down, and continues working.

Preacher: Jesus said, "If persistence wins out over a stubborn judge who cares nothing for you, will not persistence all the more win out over a gracious God who cares everything for you? Therefore, persist in your prayer! Don't lose heart! Ask repeatedly! Keep trying! Don't stop! Knock again! Make a total nuisance of yourself! Pray repeatedly! God loves you, and God will answer!"

Thus is it written in the eighteenth chapter of the Gospel according to Luke.

THE END

Chapter Five

The Call

Bible Texts: Genesis 12:1–3; Mark 1:16–20

Introduction

The most prevalent scene in the Bible is the scene in which *God calls someone*. God called Abram and Sarai. God called Jacob. God called Moses. God called Gideon. God called Deborah. God called Samuel. God called Elijah. God called Amos. God called Isaiah. God called Jeremiah. God called Mary. God called Simon and Andrew. God called James and John. God called Levi. God called Saul. The list is nearly unending. If we believe the Bible, God calls people.

You and I should expect God to call us! While we are living in a secure family in our hometown. While we are tending our father-in-law's sheep. While we are youngsters in the service of older people. After we have entered the religious sanctuary. While we are engaged in the family's business. While we are on a journey. In a variety of places, God will call us.

To leave our family home and journey into a strange land. To lead people from slavery to freedom. To perform a new task that no one has yet imagined. To prophesy to the powerful. To perform mercy and healing. To carry light into the great darkness. God will call us.

Do we listen for that to happen? Will we hear when the call comes? Are our ears and hearts tuned to the right channel? Will we respond, "Here am I, Lord, send me"?

The sermon that follows preaches that message. It employs two readers, three people from the congregation who remain at their seats, and one actor. The readers read call stories from across the Bible. The three congregation members play themselves, whoever they are. The actor plays Simon, the fisherman.

The drama maintains the theme, "God calls us!" throughout, but it passes through three movements: God calls *us*, what God calls us to *do*, and how much it will *cost*.

The thing the sermon seeks to accomplish is to have people leave worship asking themselves: What may God call *me* (or us) to do?

Location
Church sanctuary

Participants
Reader 1—A lay Bible reader from a podium
Reader 2—A lay Bible reader, from the same podium
Persons 1, 2, and 3—Typical members in the congregation
Fisherman—A man with a beard, carrying a fishing net over his
  shoulder
Preacher—In normal attire at the pulpit

Props
None

Enactment

Reader 1: The LORD said to Abram (and Sarai), "Go from your country and your kindred and your father's house to the land that I will show you." *(Gen. 12:1)*

Reader 2: As Jesus passed along the Sea of Galilee, he saw Simon and his brother Andrew casting their net into the sea—for they were fishermen. And Jesus said to them, "Follow me, and I will make you fish for people." *(Mark 1:16–17)*

Preacher stands in pulpit and addresses Person 1 in the congregation by name.

Preacher: *(name of person 1)*, did you hear that?

Person 1, surprised, stands up and peers a bit blankly at the Preacher.

Person 1: Uh, hear what, preacher?

Preacher: What *(name of reader 1)* and *(name of reader 2)* just read?

Person 1: Well, uh, yeah, I think I heard it, preacher. About Abraham, and about Simon?

Preacher: That's right. What did you hear?

Person 1: Well, uh, what was I supposed to hear?

Preacher: The Lord called them.

Person 1: Yeah, I heard that. God called Abram and Sarai to leave their family and go to an unknown place. And called Simon and Andrew to leave their fishing nets and follow.

Preacher: Thank you, *(name of reader 1)*! Well done. And did you hear anything else?

Person 1: Naw, preacher, as far as I could tell, that was it.

Preacher: Did you hear anything about yourself?

Person 1: It wasn't about me; it was a story from the Bible.

Preacher: If God called those people, what else might God do?

Person 1: Aw, come on, preacher, I'm just a pharmacist *(or a different occupation)*; things like that don't happen to me.

Preacher: Are you sure?

Person 1: Well, they never have. I just fill prescriptions.

Preacher: The way I hear those readings, they are saying that the Lord will call you and me too. Somehow, sometime. It's God's character! God calls people to do what God wants done. It's all over the Bible. You can't miss it! And God will call us! We may be an obscure family living near the mouth of the Tigris River, or we may be fisherman on the Sea of Galilee, or we may run a drug store. That part can vary. What doesn't vary is that it will happen. God will call. The only thing we don't know is when and where.

Person 1 sits down. Person 2 stands up.

Person 2: Call us to do what, preacher?

Reader 1: The Lord said to Moses, "I will send you to Pharaoh, to bring my people, the Israelites, out of Egypt." *(Exod. 3:7,10)*

Preacher: Maybe to liberate people from slavery.

Reader 2: He went up to the mountain and called to him those whom he wanted, and they came to him. And he appointed twelve, whom he also named apostles, to be with him, and to be sent out to proclaim the message, and to have authority to cast out demons. *(Mark 3:13–15)*

Preacher: Maybe to preach, maybe to heal.

Reader 1: I am a herdsman, and a dresser of sycamore trees, and the LORD took me from following the flock, and the LORD said to me, "Go prophesy to my people Israel." *(Amos 7:14–15)*

Preacher: Maybe to get your own people to see what is right in front of their eyes.

Reader 2: He said to a man with a withered hand, "Stretch out your hand." He stretched it out, and his hand was restored. *(Mark 3:5)*

Preacher: Maybe to restore withered hands, or withered lives.

Reader 1: I heard the voice of the LORD saying, "Whom shall I send, and who will go for us?" And I said, "Here am I; send me!" *(Isa. 6:8)*

Preacher: Maybe to proclaim difficult words to people whose ears are stopped up.

Person 2: Preacher, I'm just a *(states his/her occupation)*. God calls special people, people with religious abilities, not people like me.

Reader 1: Moses answered God, "But suppose they do not believe me or listen to me, but say, 'The LORD did not appear to you!'" *(Exod. 4:1)*

Preacher: We're not ever ready when God calls. We're not up to it, but God calls us anyway.

Person 2: But I don't know God that well. I come to church some and listen to you preach, but I'm just not that religious.

Reader 2: Moses answered God, "If I go to Israel and say, 'The God of your ancestors spoke to me,' they will ask, 'How have you come to know God so well?'" *(paraphrase, Exod. 3:13)*

Preacher: We don't ever know God well enough. We're not ever as religious as we should be. But God calls us anyway.

Person 2: You're asking me to listen for a voice that's not there. How am I supposed to hear that kind of thing? I've never heard God speak to anyone.

Reader 1: Moses answered, "But suppose they do not believe me or listen to me, but say, 'The Lord did not appear to you.'" *(Exod. 4:1)*

Preacher: God doesn't send words out of a cloud in English. God has other ways of speaking. But God still calls us.

Person 2: I've just never been good at religious things. I get tongue-tied when I talk in public. I can't sing. I never know what to say to people when they ask me about a problem.

Reader 2: Moses said to the Lord, "O my Lord, I have never been eloquent, neither in the past nor even now that you have spoken to your servant; I am slow of speech and slow of tongue."

Preacher: No, we may not be Billy Graham or Martin Luther King, Jr. But God calls us anyway.

Person 2 sits down. Person 3 stands up.

Person 3: Well, now, I'm pretty busy already. Just how much is God going to ask of me? I work about fifty hours a week. I go to the kids' baseball and soccer games. I work out in the gym to try to keep myself healthy. I play a game of golf on the weekend. I try to spend some social time with friends. I have three favorite night-time television programs that I don't ever miss. I come to church.

Preacher: You're a busy person, aren't you?

Person 3: Yes, and I don't know where I'm going to fit anything else. I'm spoken for already. How much do you think God is going to ask for?

Preacher: How much is God going to ask for? That's a good question. I wonder where we can find the answer.

Fisherman enters the sanctuary, making his way from one place to another. He has not come to be part of the conversation but is just passing through. He carries a fishing net over his shoulder, wears a fishing hat, and has a beard.

Preacher: Good morning, sir. Are you a fisherman?

The Fisherman pauses, looks at the Preacher and at Person 3.

Fisherman: Well, I used to be.

Preacher: Maybe you can help us with a question.

Fisherman: I'll try. What is it?

Preacher: My friend here wants to know: When God calls, how much is God going to ask for? He's a pretty busy man already, and he's wondering if he is going to have anything left to give. Can you help us with that question?

Fisherman: Why, yes, I can help you with the question.

Preacher: Well, tell us. When God calls, how much is God going to ask for?

Fisherman: Are you sure you want to know?

Person 3: Yes, we want to know.

Fisherman looks at the Preacher, looks at Person 3, then looks back at the Preacher.

Fisherman: EVERYTHING!

Person 3: Everything?

Fisherman: EVERYTHING!

Fisherman continues where he was going and disappears. Person 3 sits down.

Preacher: God called Abram and Sarai. God called Moses. God called Deborah. God called Amos. God called Isaiah. God called Mary. God called Simon and Andrew. God called Saul.

God is going to call us too! It's not a matter of whether; it's a matter of when. To set free the oppressed. To heal withered hands. To speak difficult words.

You can be sure! You can count on it!

Hear! Answer!

THE END

Chapter Six

Those Who Call Light Darkness and Darkness Light

Bible Texts: Genesis 1:1–5; Isaiah 5:18–24

Introduction

Genesis 1 attributes enormous creative power to *words*. God speaks a word, "Let there be light." With that word, light comes into being, and the light is "good" (meaning: infused with the unparalleled quality that the Creator intended). God speaks, "Let there be a dome in the midst of the waters, and let it separate the waters from the waters." With that word, a dome comes into being, and the dome is "good." God speaks, "Let the waters be gathered together and dry land appear." With that word, the waters are gathered together and dry land appears, and it is "good." God creates with words. There is, in the Bible, no more powerful force anywhere than *God's words*.

And one of the miracles of creation is that God chooses to share this power with human beings! God places in our mouths the capacity to create by speaking. God sets on our tongues this enormous capability.

When I was in junior high school, I played first base on a sandlot baseball team. Our team gave names to several of our players, names that highlighted what they did best. Our center fielder was called "speedy," because he could shag nearly anything hit his way. Our right fielder was called "moose," because he hit so many balls into the trees in the deep outfield. Our third baseman was called "pepper," because his chatter kept the whole team alert and alive.

The team had a problem with me. I was not an overly good athlete, not particularly strong, and not fast. But I did have one ability they came to value. I could lean half way across the infield from first base and turn some pretty rotten throws into outs. More than once, I kept some infielder teammate from being charged with a throwing error. The name they gave me, therefore, was "stretch."

In the years ahead, that single word did more to create me than anyone could ever know. It stated my primary value to the team. It gave me a strong sense of belonging. It told me I was especially good at something. It gave me confidence and made me work harder. Years later, I would still feel pride when I ran into an ex-teammate and he addressed me that way.

There is nothing more creative than a well-chosen word, just as there is also nothing more destructive than a spitefully chosen word.

Two different commandments in Exodus 20 urge us to use words truthfully and well. "Thou shalt not take the name of the Lord thy God in vain"; or, thou shalt not use God's name as a theological justification for your opinions and prejudices. And, "Thou shalt not bear false witness against thy neighbor," or, thou shalt not use words to convey falsehood about other people.

Several Biblical witnesses become powerfully distressed that we human beings take this marvelous language power God has given us and misuse it so badly.

Isaiah says, "Woe to those who call evil good and good evil, who put darkness for light and light for darkness, who put bitter for sweet and sweet for bitter." Woe to those who fashion words to convey desired image rather than actual truth, to the spin specialists whose only purpose is to use words to get us to believe what they want us to believe, to those who employ language to call things exactly the opposite of what they actually are.

"Woe to . . ." means: You will be overcome by consequences too awful to describe. The fundamental fabric of your community will be torn apart by this activity.

ᘒᘌᘒᘌᘒ—ᘌᘒᘌᘒᘌ

In our society, "growing up"—changing from childhood into adulthood—includes learning what speech is not to be believed at all, what language is to be automatically discounted. A mature adult knows what the list includes: what many strangers say when they stop us in public, what far too many politicians say while they are campaigning for office, and what we hear in a great deal of advertising. Beyond these categories, we have to learn which language to trust and which not to trust, how to develop a third ear for discerning truthless language when we hear it.

The sermon drama that follows is intended to unveil our deceitful use of language and to call us toward a more faithful employment of God's sacred gift.

Location
Church sanctuary

Participants
Reader—A lay Bible reader
Preacher—In normal attire at the pulpit

Panel One
A young couple—dressed for their own wedding
A clergyperson—also dressed for a wedding

Panel Two
A salesperson

Panel Three
A worshiper—dressed appropriately for worship, who is wearing
    some prominent, easily visible green
An "attack dog"—someone who can accuse, who can caricature
    demeaningly

Panel Four
A teacher
Four or five children—ages seven through ten

Panel Five
Two businesspeople—one a bit older, the other a bit younger,
    both dressed for the office during a work day

Props
Panel One
Bouquet of flowers

Panel Two
An old, rusty, dilapidated bicycle
Cloth large enough to cover bicycle

Panel Four
Five pieces of brightly colored poster board, each with a label
    across the bottom:
Black board—label: "white"
White board—label: "black"
Yellow board—label: "red"

Green board—label: "yellow"
Red board—label: "green"

Panel Five
An office desk with a chair or two

Enactment

Reader: *(Genesis 1:1–5; Isaiah 5:18–24)*

Preacher: God said, "Let there be light." And, with that single word, light
came into being. And God inspected the light that God's word
had created, and God declared the light "good." "Good" meaning, infused with the unparalleled quality that its Creator
intended.

God said, "Let there be a firmament to separate the
waters." And, with that single word, there was a firmament
to separate the waters. God inspected the firmament God's
word had created, and God declared the firmament
"good."

God said, "Let there be dry land." And, with that single
word, the waters gathered together and the dry land
appeared. And God inspected the dry land that God's word
had created, and God declared the dry land "good."

God said, "Let there be a man and a woman." And, with
that single word, a man and a woman were created. God
looked at the man and the woman and declared that they
were "very good," precisely what their Creator intended.

And then God did a magical thing. God took the language God had used in creating the creation, and God
placed that language in the mouths of the man and the
woman. To give them creative power as well. The power
to create relationship. The power to bring order. The
power to remember. The power to hope. The power to do
all the marvelous things language empowers men and
women to do. God gave this power to the man and the
woman.

And God said to them, "This language I give you is
sacred! My precious gift! Use it carefully! Use it wisely! If
you do so, it will spread good throughout your community.

It will provide you with the greatest of blessings. But if you use my language unfaithfully, deceitfully, manipulatively, it will curse you! It will drive your community apart and destroy your relationship.

Reader: From Proverbs 10. Whoever speaks with integrity, walks securely. Whoever speaks perversity is destined to fall. The mouth of the righteous is a fountain of life, but the mouth of the wicked is a cover for violence. The tongue of the righteous is choice silver; the words of the wicked are useless trash.

Panel One

Young couple in wedding clothing quickly appears at the front of the sanctuary. She is carrying a bouquet. Clergyperson dressed to lead a wedding also appears. They stand facing one another. They pick up in the middle of the wedding ceremony.

Clergyperson: In joy and in sorrow.

Couple: *(together)* In joy and in sorrow.

Clergyperson: In plenty and in want.

Couple: In plenty and in want.

Clergyperson: In sickness and in health.

Couple: In sickness and in health.

Clergyperson: In youth and in age.

Couple: In youth and in age.

Clergyperson: In harmony and in discord.

Couple: In harmony and in discord.

Clergyperson: Until death do us part.

Couple: Until death do us part.

Preacher: God said to the man and the woman, "This language I am giving you is sacred! My precious possession! Use it carefully! Use it wisely! If you do so, it will bless you. It will provide you with the greatest blessing you can find."

Couple and clergyperson disappear quickly.

Panel Two

From another direction, the Salesperson appears at the front of the sanctuary. He/she removes a cloth covering off an object that has been sitting there throughout: an old, dilapidated bicycle. He/she begins expounding the virtues of the bicycle to the congregation.

Salesperson: Sparkling before your eyes! A ready companion waiting to step into your life! Consider the joy the two of you can have together! Up the hills, down the lanes! It will get to know you, and you will get to know it! A perfect friend that will travel every road with you. Warmth waiting to happen! This is the fulfillment of your wishes, the answer to your prayers. Look at it: It is begging you to make it your own!

Salesperson disappears.

Reader: From Isaiah 5 (RSV). Woe to you who call evil good and good evil, who put darkness for light and light for darkness, who put bitter for sweet and sweet for bitter.

Preacher: "Woe to . . . ," in the Bible, means: There is no description to match the results of this sin. You will be overcome by consequences too awful to describe. The fabric of your community will be torn apart. "Woe to you who call good evil and evil good."

Panel Three

Worshiper moves slowly down an aisle of the church toward the front. Attack Dog appears from another direction, looks at worshiper, snaps to alertness and begins his/her tirade.

Attack Dog: *(gesturing at Worshiper but addressing congregation)* Do you understand what is happening here, ladies and gentlemen? This woman *(or man)* is running for a position on the governing board of this church. She *(he)* wants to be one of your leaders. Do you realize what a disaster that would be? Oh, she's *(he's)* friendly enough and puts herself *(himself)* across as one of US, but let me tell you. . . .

Three years ago, when my husband was running for the school board, she *(he)* was one of those people in our neighborhood association who voted to declare the grassy triangle at the end of her street off limits to political signs. Can you believe that? She *(he)* called it, "maintaining the integrity of the green space." Well, I call it, "curtailing the freedom of speech of law-abiding citizens!" All for a few silly blades of grass! I'll never forget that.

Look at that green she's *(he's)* wearing! That's her *(his)* way of pushing her *(his)* agenda on us!

Think about it. What kind of church leader will she *(he)* make? If someone like that gets elected, the first governing board meeting will be a rally to tear down the announcement board in front of the church because it disturbs her *(his)* idea of good landscaping. And that would only be the beginning.

Worshiper moves near Attack Dog, oblivious to all that has been said.

Attack Dog: Oh, here she *(he)* comes. "Good morning, *(worshiper name)*, so nice to be worshiping with you today!

Worshiper and Attack Dog disappear.

Reader: Woe to you who call evil good and good evil, who put darkness for light and light for darkness, who put bitter for sweet and sweet for bitter.

Preacher: All of us have done good things and less good things. All of us are made of better qualities and worse qualities. All of us have had moments we are proud of and moments we would prefer to forget. Selectively highlighting the negative drives good people into the shadows, undermines trust, destroys community. Respect, for both colleagues and adversaries, builds community.

Panel Four

Teacher and Students appear at the front of the sanctuary. The Students sit down in a group mostly with their backs to the congregation. The Teacher faces Students and congregation. He/she carries the five pieces of colored poster board. The Teacher's manner is important. He/she is not an evil person, not there to teach deception, not there to lead the class into something bad. The Teacher is doing the class a favor: teaching them how

language and words are sometimes used in the adult world into which they are grow-
ing. The Teacher is their friend, honestly delivering a lesson in future reality.

> **Teacher:** *(addressing students)* Today, students, we are going to study our colors.

Teacher sets the five pieces of poster board so they are clearly visible both to Students and to congregation.

> **Teacher:** Now, I know that you learned your colors several years ago. But you are old enough now for your next lesson. Let's begin with a review.

Teacher points to white board.

> **Teacher:** Let's all say it together.
>
> **All:** White.

Teacher points to black board.

> **Teacher:** All together.
>
> **All:** Black.

Teacher points to yellow board.

> **Teacher:** Together.
>
> **All:** Yellow.

Teacher points to green board.

> **Teacher:** As one.
>
> **All:** Green.

Teacher points to red board.

> **Teacher:** All together.
>
> **All:** Red.

Teacher: Very good. Now, here is your next lesson. Sometimes you need to be able to see things differently from this.

Teacher points to white board.

Teacher: Sometimes this is black. B-l-a-c-k. You need to be able to think of it as black. You need to be able to see it as black. Say it with me.

All: Black.

Teacher points to black board.

Teacher: And sometimes this is white. The color of snow. The color of milk. It's important that you be able to see it as white. Say it with me.

All: White.

Teacher: Good, I think you're getting it.

Teacher points to yellow board.

Teacher: And sometimes this is red. You will have to retrain yourself to think this way, but you can get it. You need to know when this needs to be red. Say it with me.

All: Red.

Teacher: Good.

Teacher points to green board.

Teacher: And sometimes this is yellow. Y-e-l-l-o-w. The bright, cheery color. It is important that, when it is necessary, you be able to agree that this is yellow. Repeat it with me.

All: Yellow.

Teacher: You are learning very well.

Teacher points to red board.

Teacher: And sometimes this is green. The color of grass. Your senses may tell you otherwise, but there will be times in your life when this will need to be green. It is important that you understand the necessity of being able to see it as green. Say it with me.

All: Green.

Teacher: Class, you are doing quite well. Now, review with me.

Teacher points to white board.

Teacher: We all know that this is white. Say it.

All: White.

Teacher points to black board.

Teacher: And that this is black. Say it.

All: Black.

Teacher points to yellow board.

Teacher: And that this is yellow. Say it.

All: Yellow.

Teacher points to green board.

Teacher: And that this is green. All together.

All: Green.

Teacher points to red board.

Teacher: And that this is red. Say it.

All: Red.

Teacher points to white board.

Teacher: But today's lesson is that in the world around you this can also be black. Say it.

All: Black.

Teacher points to black board.

> **Teacher**: And this can be white. Say it.
>
> **All**: White.

Teacher points to yellow board.

> **Teacher**: And this can be red. Say it.
>
> **All**: Red.

Teacher points to green board.

> **Teacher**: And this can be yellow. Say it.
>
> **All**: Yellow.

Teacher points to red board.

> **Teacher**: And this can be green. Say it.
>
> **All**: Green.
>
> **Teacher**: Class, you have taken a major step here today in making your way into adulthood. I want to congratulate you on a job well done!

Teacher and students exit quickly.

> **Reader**: Woe to you who call evil good and good evil, who put darkness for light and light for darkness, who put bitter for sweet and sweet for bitter.
>
> **Preacher**: If white is black and black is white, if yellow is red and green is yellow and red is green, who can tell what to believe? Growing up in our world has become *really* complicated.

Panel Five

Older and younger businesspeople appear at front. Desk has been situated in a usable location with chairs close by. Desk belongs to Younger; Older has entered Younger's office space.

Older: That Perryman agreement really looks good. Sounds like every-one is going to be happy with that one. You did a good job on it. I know it took a lot of hard work.

Younger: I was really pleased with the outcome. They are good people to work with.

Older: Did you get Perryman's signature?

Younger: *(spoken very strongly and distinctly)* When you're working with Perryman, you don't need his signature. All you need is his word.

After a moment's sink-in time, Older and Younger exit quickly.

Reader: Truthful lips endure forever. A lying tongue lasts only a moment. Lying tongues are an abomination to the Lord. Those who speak faithfully are God's delight.

Preacher: "You don't need his signature. All you need is his word."

God did a magical, mysterious thing. God took the language God had used in creating the creation, and God placed that language in the mouths of the man and the woman. So that they could possess God's creative power.

And God said to the man and the woman, "This language I am giving you is sacred! My precious possession! Use it carefully! Use it wisely! If you do so, it will spread good throughout your community. It will bestow upon you the greatest of blessings. But if you use it unfaithfully, deceitfully, manipulatively, it will curse you! It will drive you apart from one another and destroy your community."

"I call heaven and earth to witness against you today that I have set before you life and death, blessing and curse. Choose life so that you and your descendants may live." *(Deut. 30:19 RSV)*

THE END

Chapter Seven

He Is Risen!

Bible Text: Luke 24:1–12

Introduction

Easter morning proclaims that God raised Jesus from the dead. It also proclaims that God can raise us from the dead, not only into another life but also into this life.

Gender hierarchy, the belief that one gender is to dominate and rule the other, brings death to a community. God can raise us from this death.

My anger against another person, especially if it is extended anger, is death, not death to the other person but to me. God can raise me from this death.

Community violence, the disfiguring of one another with guns, is death. God can raise us from this death.

Not to notice the people around us every day, not to hear their voices, not to receive their stories—usually because we are too busy and too highly scheduled—is death. God can raise us from this death.

We suffer all kinds of deaths while we are still living. Easter morning proclaims that God's power can raise us from these deaths.

The sermon drama that follows begins and ends by proclaiming the resurrection power of God. In the middle are five specific situations from which God can resurrect us. Some of the material is quite specific to my own congregation. I have, nevertheless, included it because it illustrates what can be done. You may wish to adapt this with situations from your congregation.

Location
Church sanctuary

Participants
Panel One
Two preachers—In normal attire, preferably from two different pulpits

Panel Two
Three women capable of conveying their excitement—In normal modern dress
Four men—disciples, one of them Peter, in normal modern dress

Panel Three
Two auto drivers—both dressed in t-shirt and jeans

Panel Five
Refugee—male, casual modern dress

Panel Six
Lonely woman—a woman who appears to have wrapped herself inside herself
Child—an innocent-looking four-year-old girl
At least four passerby adults—In normal attire

Panel Seven
Hospital patient—male

Props
One chair at front

Enactment

Panel One

Preacher 1: This morning there is good news! "He is not here; he is risen!" Thus spoke two men in dazzling clothing inside his tomb. "Why do you seek the living among the dead? Remember, how he told you that he would be handed over to sinners, and be crucified, and on the third day rise." The great stone has been rolled back.

The place where they laid him is vacant. The tomb is empty. He is risen!

A day like no other! A day on which the Lord has acted! A day that will mark all other days.

God's power moves among us! God's spirit with us. The power to break chains. The power to free slaves. The power to make old things new. The power to bring life from death.

Panel Two

Preacher 2: The women who had gone to the tomb ran back into Jerusalem to tell his disciples.

Three Women come running into the front of the sanctuary, very excited. At the same time, Four Men appear, much less animated. The Three Women address the Four Men.

Woman 1: Hear us! His tomb is empty; he is gone!

Woman 2: Two men in dazzling clothes stood where he had been! They said, "He is not here; he has risen! He is gone!"

Woman 3: We saw it! We went there with spices!

Preacher 2: The disciples heard the women, but paid little attention.

Man 1: Yeah, sure, we understand.

Man 2: Women get excited, don't they. They see things.

Man 3: Yeah, they imagine a lot.

Man 1: Two dazzling young men!

Man 2: That, frankly, is what they've been looking for all their lives.

Preacher 2: The disciples, Luke tells us, dismissed the entire matter, considering it "an idle tale" of women.

Except for one disciple, Peter, who decided to look for himself.

Man 4, who has not spoken, has a questioning look. He finally leaves the group quietly and heads away.

Preacher 2: A good thing! Otherwise the First Church of Jerusalem would have completely missed the resurrection of Jesus Christ. The moment of God's great act, and God's disciples paying no attention.

The power of God comes to raise us from the dead. From the hierarchies that cause some of us to disregard others. From our own feelings of superiority. From that brush-off—"Oh, women!" Such things cause death in the human community! God raises us today to new life.

Panel Three

Preacher 1: The street was too narrow for the two cars to pass each other. Cars parked on both sides, and only one lane up the middle. I don't know what had happened up to this point, but the two vehicles were at an impasse, stopped in that middle lane, facing each other, each waiting for the other to back up, neither budging. The predictable was beginning to happen. The drivers were leaning out of their doors, glaring at each other.

The Two Drivers appear at the front, one from one side, the other from the other. They halt, facing each other. Looking. Glaring.

Preacher 1: They started muttering comments, insults, smears.

Driver 1 speaks in pantomime. Driver 2 replies in the same manner. The first speaks more strongly. The second replies—all in pantomime.

Preacher 1: One insulted the other's mother.

Drive 1 waves his fist and hurls an obvious insult.

Preacher 1: The other equated the one to the equine posterior.

Driver 2 waves both fists and shouts even more vigorously—all pantomime.

Preacher 1: Their anger was spilling out over the street. There was the distinct feel that most of their anger had started before they encountered each other, that they were anger waiting to happen.

Driver 1 and Driver 2 gesture angrily and violently toward each other, mouthing great intensity.

Preacher 1: Products of Rush Limbaugh, or talk radio, or anger-rap. Or maybe something else.

Driver 1 and Driver 2, after flourishes of anger, exit, each obviously seething inside over the encounter.

Preacher 1: The anger is rising, my friends. We hear it on the streets. We hear it in music. We hear it in offices. We hear it in political campaigns. "Hate him!" "Despise her!" "Destroy them!"—it is a daily litany.

The power of God comes today to raise us from the dead. From the tempests that blow in our heads. From the storms that rage across our hearts. From our own anger.

To create on the wrathful sea a great calm. Anger is death!—death to the one who is angry. God brings life!

Panel Four

Preacher 2: I am working on a project. To collect guns, guns that have been removed from the streets. Guns that would otherwise be out there threatening people. Buy-back guns. Turn-in guns. We're trying to collect several hundred of them. We're going to disfigure them, bend them, warp them, twist them, impair them, wreck them—do to them what they would otherwise do to us.

And then we are going to find an artist who will weld them together into a sculpture: a huge plowshare. A testimony to God's promise. "They shall beat their swords into plowshares, and their spears into pruning hooks. Nation shall not lift up sword against nation, neither shall they learn war anymore. But each shall sit under his own vine and under her own fig tree, and none shall make them afraid." We are going to plant that plowshare solidly in a public place as living testimony.

Amid the fear we create, God promises confidence. Amid the violence we create, God promises peace. Amid the death we create, God promises life. Today is the day on which God acts.

Panel Five

Preacher 1: The time is mid-morning on a weekday. I get out of my car parked on Cherokee Road, a few steps from where we are now. A group of young men stands on the sidewalk outside the church office, talking among themselves. A couple of them are smoking; one is drinking a Mountain Dew. Veering slightly from the route into the office, I approach them. They become aware of me.

"How is your English?" I ask, addressing them directly, wondering if any of them will know what I am saying. Several of them look perplexed, trying to understand, checking with one another. One, however, looks straight at me.

Refugee walks to the front, stands facing the congregation.

Preacher 1: With a kind of joshing smile, he says:

Refugee: *(smiling in a friendly way, speaking in a thick Balkan accent, enunciating each word distinctly, dragging the vowels heavily, and holding up his two flattened hands in front of him, almost but not quite together in a clapping position)* A leeetle beeet.

Preacher 1: I stand there thinking of where he came from: shelling, gunfire, bloodshed, killing. Crowds of refugees moving down a road; a hectic border crossing. He seems now so everyday, so normal. And yet his words and his manner express the determination that has brought him to this place. "I did not get myself out of Kosovo so that we could get here and fail," he is saying.

The look of humble determination shows on the Refugee's face.

Preacher 1: "I am not a person who buckles. I will someday stand right beside you as your neighbor." I read it in his face and body. And then he speaks again.

Refugee: *(holding up his hands in the same way as before, close together)* A leeetle beeet now. But soon *(his hands jump apart in a sweeping gesture)*, A LOT!"

Preacher 1: I know that I am watching a resurrection. The power of God at work!

Panel Six

Lonely Woman makes her way to the front and sits in a chair, facing the congregation.

Preacher 2: The room was too quiet for Sarah to hear anything. She had been alone so long, even the voices in her own head were silenced. There was nothing. No one.

Four Passerby Adults walk past, quipping, talking with one another. They notice the Woman, look for a moment inquisitively, but move by.

Preacher 2:   The past, the reasons for this total removal, had long before been lost to view. Sarah didn't know why. Anyone looking in from the outside could only speculate. And speculate they did, ad nauseum. But no one dared to break down the wall that kept a human heart from loving.

Three more Passerby Adults come by, and the Child, holding the hand of one of the adults.

Preacher 2:   Until Meg.

Child notices Lonely Woman, regards her, hesitates, but then, with resolve, turns loose of the adult's hand and goes to her.

Preacher 2:   Until a small child, recognizing in her innocence something that too many in their intelligence have forgotten, reached in.

Child arrives beside Lonely Woman, tentatively and softly places her hands on Lonely Woman's lap.

Preacher 2:   And through, and down, and around.

Child reaches across and hugs Lonely Woman securely around the waist, nestling her head into Lonely Woman's body.

Preacher 2:   And touched a shaking hand, calming the storm, breaking down a wall. In this simple act, a touch, others began to realize, to remember, that the fullness of their lives does not reside in their own happiness, but is to be found only as they seek the happiness of others.

The power of God to raise us from the death of separation and self-centered individualism. To create community. To enhance and deepen life with one another. To free the love that emanates from every person.

Isolation, inflicted or chosen, is death! God brings life!

All exit.

Panel Seven

Patient, a man with a hospital gown over his regular clothes and with several tubes taped to his arms and a bandage wrapped around his head, walks slowly to the front. He is carrying a manila folder full of papers, a cell phone, and a laptop computer. He addresses the congregation.

Patient: It's a miracle. Lying right here in this room, I have discovered a new world. It is wonderful. It is marvelous.

I've always been devoted to my work, a high-intensity guy.

Patient offers the things he is carrying as evidence, then sets them down.

Patient: But I have made a new discovery in the past two weeks. Rodney, over there in the next bed *(points to an invisible roommate)*. Rodney is a jazz musician. Plays the night spots downtown. A gentle, kind-hearted guy; weaves magic with his clarinet. Loves to make people feel good. Loves to get a crowd in tune. Rodney has told me his stories, and they are fascinating.

And Ruby, there *(points toward another invisible figure in another direction)*. Ruby comes in here every day with a mop and a dust pan to make sure this room stays clean. Ruby has four children. Two of them are young twins. One of them plays high school basketball but probably isn't that good. Another one loves to write and is trying to get a scholarship to take creative writing in college. Ruby reads—especially mysteries and southern novels—but the main thing she is trying to do is give her kids a lot better start in life than she had. Ruby is filled with spirit, comes in here singing gospel songs every day. A wonderful woman; you can't imagine how inspiring she is to me.

And Carla, that nurse who was just in here. Carla grew up really poor. But she got herself through nursing school, mostly by pure determination. And now she is darned good at what she does, and she is also a sweet, kind human being. Carla just makes me feel good every morning when she walks in that door.

I have discovered a magnificent world. It's been here around me all the time, and I finally saw it.

Panel Eight

Preacher 1: Today there is good news! He is risen; he is not here. The stone has been rolled back; the place where they laid him is vacant. The tomb is empty. He has risen!

Blow the trumpets of victory! God's power moves among us! God's spirit moves in us! The power to break chains. To free slaves. To make old things new. To bring life from death.

Hallelujah! The Lord God omnipotent reigneth! Amen.

THE END

Chapter Eight

Additional Suggestions

My main wish in this book is to encourage you to create your own sermon drama. You have the Bible. You have your knowledge of its stories. You have imagination. You have familiarity with your sanctuary space, and you know what will communicate best with your congregation.

I devote this final chapter to some additional brief ideas, hoping to encourage you.

It takes work. Sticking with the traditional monologue is simpler, easier. But I encourage you to be creative yourself. It will revolutionize the way you think about sermons.

Set a high standard for yourself. Anyone can concoct a cute little skit that people will enjoy. That won't do. Challenge yourself to make your sermon drama interesting and substantial. Interesting, in that the hearer will say, "I never thought of it that way before." Substantial, in that it presents God's word to us, Christ's call.

Here are some ideas.

The Stilling of the Storm
Mark 4:35–41

The chief dynamic in this story is the movement from the raging watery chaos to the "great calm," the transition from loud uproar to stillness. We are invited to stand with the disciples in awe before the One who thus controls the waters, the One who is capable of saying to the storm, "Peace! Be still!" If the traditional understanding of the Gospel of Mark is correct—that it was addressed to an early Christian church that was being battered by storms of Roman persecution—a drama could depict an early house church meeting, held in secret, where the travails of the community were discussed but where this story was read to calm and fortify the faithful. The message would be the overall message of the Gospel of Mark: stand firm! Endure to the end! Remain faithful!

The Blind Man at Bethsaida
Mark 8:22–26

Here is a simple story, easily enacted, about a blind man Jesus has to touch twice before the man is made whole, just as Jesus has to touch us many times to make us whole. The best New Testament illustration of the point of this story is Simon Peter, who has to be "converted" at least four times in the scope of Luke and Acts.

The Feeding of the Five Thousand
Mark 6:30–44

Several actors could enact briefly the reaction of disciples as they return from taking up broken pieces. They carry baskets piled high with leftovers, and they look at one another in awe, wondering, "How could this happen? Who is he?" It is God, of course, who provides manna in the desert and quail in the wilderness.

Cain and Abel
Genesis 4:1–16

A single-actor sermon drama could depict Cain in the role of the classic older brother, thinking aloud over the gross injustice done to him by his parents and his resulting motive for killing his younger brother. The drama could weave the ancient story and the modern dynamic into a single fabric. There has never been an older sibling who understood why mom and dad offered such outrageously preferential treatment to a little punk. The Genesis editor used this story to depict how sin grows in us, from the simple ill of disobedience to murder.

Lamech
Genesis 4:23–24

A single actor could depict Lamech arriving at home in the evening boasting to his wives about the argument he had with a man in the bar.

The man had insulted him and struck him. But he, Lamech, slew the man with his fists. He now feels vastly superior for having avenged seventy-sevenfold the wrong done against him—far more even than Cain who avenged the wrong done against him sevenfold.

In this story, human ill grows from murder to vengeful murder, murder that the murderer thoroughly enjoys. Lamech is that element in us that is satisfied only by asserting our ascendency over would-be competitors.

This passage can be developed in relation to Matthew 18:21–22 in which Jesus tells his disciples that they are to forgive not seven times but seventy-seven times, thereby reversing the spirit of vengeance that Lamech unleashed upon the earth and replacing it with an even greater spirit of forgiveness.

A second actor could relate the story of a forgiveness scene as gripping as Lamech's vengeance scene, of someone who forgave under truly extraordinary circumstances.

Amos and Amaziah, The Priest at Bethel
Amos 7:10–17

A two-person drama could enact the interchange between Amos and Amaziah, the priest at the religious sanctuary in Bethel. The priest, paid and fed by the king, represents the viewpoint that all is well in the kingdom of Israel, that there is great prosperity, and that religion is experiencing a strong burst of popularity, and that under such conditions no one should criticize the king's leadership.

Amos speaks the word God spoke to him: that great numbers of God's people are destitute and starving, sharing in none of the prosperity, returned to the oppression and slavery from which God delivered them in Egypt. The priest tells Amos to take his critical words elsewhere! Amos says he would not utter a word except at God's instruction.

Hosea in the Bosom of God
Hosea 11:1–9

Hosea is the first person in the Bible (Jeremiah will stand in the same tradition, and John, the Gospel writer, will provide a variation) who sees himself as dwelling in the bosom of God; that is, literally sitting on God's lap to hear and perceive God's thoughts, feelings, and emotions and then reporting them to earth. We have all, at some age, sat on someone's lap, with head nestled to chest, and we can remember how much of that person we discerned. The Gospel writer John will later see himself as the disciple who sat in the bosom of Jesus, the one who discerned Jesus' heart and emotions.

Hosea 11:1–9 is the classic passage. A single actor could depict Hosea freshly returned from sitting on God's lap and reporting what he/she experienced. The passage (vv. 1–4) begins with God's intense frustration over the waywardness of God's child, Israel. God had loved that child, tended that child, cared for that child. But Israel, in return, sacrificed to the Baals and burned incense to idols—and all that that implies for ethical behavior. God decides (vv. 5–7) to return Israel to Egypt, to throw them back into slavery, to stop being their parent, to withdraw and disappear, to let the evil they love so much possess them. But after this fit of frustration, God realizes (vv. 8–9) that it cannot happen, that God cannot cast God's own child into slavery, that this is not in God's heart as a possibility. Because, in God's words, "I am God, and no mortal, the Holy One in your midst, and I will not come in wrath." Human beings might do such a thing, but God cannot.

This passage cries out to be enacted by someone capable of doing it well. It is a commentary on what second Isaiah will later say,

> My thoughts are not your thoughts,
> nor are your ways my ways, says the LORD.
> For as the heavens are higher than the earth,
> so are my ways higher than your ways,
> and my thoughts than your thoughts.
> (Isa. 55:8–9)

The God of the Bible is repeatedly, invariably, endlessly, and startlingly bigger than we think.

The Syrophoenician Woman
Mark 7:24–30

A single actress could, as the Syrophoenician woman, reflect on her encounter with Jesus. The woman had sought Jesus' help in casting a demon out of her sick daughter. She was desperate! Jesus replied that God had sent him to bring healing to God's people, not to foreigners. To say this, he quoted a popular saying of his time, one of those tidbits of common wisdom that was oft repeated through his culture, "Let the children be fed first, for it is not fair to take the children's food and throw it to the dogs." This saying is entirely analogous to the popular saying in our time, "Charity begins at home."

For the woman, however, her sick child transcended popular philosophy, social division, cultural difference, and everything else. She was desperate to have her child exorcised. In her reply to Jesus, she ignored the put-down in his words—the implication that she and her daughter were analogous to dogs. She even accepted the role of "dog," but then called upon Jesus to have a greater theology than the one implied in his words: "Sir, even the dogs under the table eat the children's crumbs." In other words, "Does not your God love more than simply Israelite children?"

Mark gives us no insight into Jesus' mind at this moment. But it must have been analogous to Judah's mind when the pregnant Tamar produced Judah's signet and cord as he was about to have her stoned (Gen. 38 RSV). Judah said, "She is more righteous than I," an *amazing* statement for a patriarch of Israel, especially in reference to a woman. Jesus said, "For saying that, you may go—the demon has left your daughter," carrying the same impact. Jesus was affirming the woman's theology: that God does love more than just Israelite children, that God's love is a great deal more universal than ours is.

The actress's reflection could convey her anxiety over her daughter, but then tell of her quick but carefully formulated response to Jesus' words. She could then reflect on his having listened to her and taken her so seriously in a culture that generally did not do such a thing. She could end with a theological reflection on how God's love transcends lots of human boundaries.

Create in Me a Clean Heart
Psalm 51

A dancer or pantomimist could portray the emotion of Psalm 51 as a pastor reads and preaches the text. The mood begins with profound humility, repentance, prostration, the emotion of one who has done wrong and very much knows it. It then unfolds into supplication for renewal, and then into promise. The psalm's line, "Create in me a clean heart, O God, and put a new and right spirit within me," is the opportunity for full flowering, a joyousness born of forgiveness granted.

This psalm can be preached as a counterpoint to the cheap, vastly overused comment, "I just want to put this behind me and get on with my life," which is usually another way of saying, "I want everyone to forget what I have done and move on as if I had not done it." Our sinfulness is not a superficial matter. Neither is our renewal. Psalm 51 expresses the profundity of the entire enterprise.

Give the King Thy Justice
Psalm 72

Psalm 72 is the perfect set-up for a preacher and two proclaimers. The psalm interlaces two elements. One is a prayer to God to bless the king, to make his dominion great and his rule long. The other is a statement of the kingly conduct that will cause this to happen: that the king defends the cause of the poor and rescues the afflicted. The fact that this psalm brings these two elements into this relationship is quite strange. Normally we would think that the king's dominion would be great and his rule long if he maintains a strong and prosperous economy, he assembles a strong army, and he has connection with powerful and influential people both at home and abroad. This may be true among humans, but not so with God. God gives dominion and longevity to kings who use their royal power to defend the poor and rescue the afflicted. It is a radical notion, this preference of God for advocating for the weak.

The preacher could issue the proclamations of God's blessings on the king. The first proclaimer could ask repeatedly, "Will God grant these blessings because of the king's piety, the king's exceptional spirituality? Because of the king's connections and influence? Because of the king's military preparedness? Because of the king's great wealth?" The second proclaimer could reply repeatedly the message of the psalm: that it is because the king cares profoundly about people who live in homeless shelters, about people who spend the night under highway overpasses, about "the least of these my brothers and sisters."

These three voices can weave through one another to create the sermon.

Where Shall I Go From Your Spirit?
Psalm 139

A dancer or pantomimist could portray the wondrous marvels of this psalm as the preacher reads and/or preaches it.

"LORD, you have searched me and known me. . . ." The notion of being fully and thoroughly known, comprehended, perceived by God can be danced or mimed. This text is parallel to Paul's comment in 1 Corinthians 13:12, "Then I will know fully, even as I have been fully known." One of the paramount experiences of Biblical faith was the experience of being fully and totally listened to, regarded, known.

"Where can I go from your spirit? Or where can I flee from your presence?" A dancer can delightfully portray ascending to the heights and finding God, descending to the depths and finding God, traveling to the outer limits and still finding God.

The sermon can end with the point that it is far less critical that we know God—there are severe limits on our capacity to do that—than that God know us! Those who are fully and thoroughly known, regarded, cherished, have a place in the universe, a home, an identity, a peace that passes all understanding. Those who are not known become fugitives and wanderers upon the earth (Gen. 4:12).

Changing the Image of the Sons of God
Psalm 2; Matthew 5:9; Mark 10:35–45; Philippians 2:5–11

A dancer or pantomimist could portray the striking change the Bible develops in the concept "son of God."

A son of God (Psalm 2) originates as a master of military might, a conqueror, an invincible power figure who is able to silence the nations and bring even the most haughty under his command. That is, a son of God is one who has been given a share of God's great strength, God's thunderous power, God's capacity to rule and command decisively.

Jesus changes this image entirely. A son of God becomes a peacemaker (Matt. 5:9), a servant (Mark 10:45), not one who lords it over others but one who gives himself for others. The servant song of Philippians 2:5-11 never uses the term "son of God," but that is certainly what "equality with God" is all about.

As the sermon is developed, the dancer could move from son of God as master to son of God as servant.